Thoughts Can Heal

Denise Lynn

Find Me On Facebook:
https://www.facebook.com/authordeniselynn/

Disclaimer:

This book is not intended as a substitute for the medical advice of physicians. The reader should regularly consult a physician in matters relating to his/her health and particularly with respect to any symptoms that may require diagnosis or medical attention.

Table of Contents

Foreword

Thoughts Can Heal was inspired by my personal experience dealing with anxiety while caretaking my fiancé who had terminal cancer.

I was experiencing a type of grief called Anticipatory Grief, and the fear thoughts about losing him manifested as severe anxiety in my mind and body.

At the time I had no idea I was grieving. Heck, I had never even heard of the term "Anticipatory Grief". I had struggled with anxiety in the past, but after getting involved in yoga and meditation I could control my symptoms so I was frustrated at not being able to get a grip on it again during this time of my life.

In hindsight, of course I was anxious. The man I loved had a terminal disease. Who wouldn't be on high alert? But because I didn't know I was grieving, and that anxiety is one of the major symptoms of this type of grief, I went on a quest to better understand my mind and the power of thought. This search for understanding led me on a spiritual journey that taught me about the healing powers we have within and just how powerful our thoughts really are.

To cope with the symptoms of anxiety I started doing these daily practices and they helped me get through some of the darkest nights of my soul. Some I had been teaching my yoga students for years, others I learned from mentors and success coaches. All of them are useful. Some help calm your nervous system and the others help reprogram your subconscious mind.

I choose to see this as an opportunity to take what I experienced and use it to help others. My heart tells me now that the reason I ran to my longtime friend's side when he was diagnosed with cancer, and fell in love with him, was so I could eventually fulfill the purpose of helping others who are experiencing anxiety. There was a strong calling to run to him, and while many couldn't understand why someone would fall in love with a person who had a terminal disease, I followed my heart and it led me here.

This book is for anyone suffering from habitual negative thoughts or fear-based thoughts. It's these old patterns of thinking that need to be reprogramed in our subconscious minds. It's really that simple. The key is repetition.

Do these practices in order, or flip to one that resonates with you. There's no right or wrong. Do whatever feels good for you, but do them as often as possible to see the greatest results in your healing and in your life.

As a bonus you can apply these same practices and writing exercises to all areas of your life. They've helped me create more financial abundance, more harmony in my home, an overall feeling of gratitude and healthier relationships.

I'm forever grateful you have allowed me to be a part of your healing journey.

Truly, thoughts can heal.

Warmth and love,
Denise Lynn

Day 1: Affirmations & Repetition

Sit quietly three times today and with your non-dominant hand, write this affirmation five times: I am safe.

This exercise may seem silly and will be uncomfortable at first, but after a few days it will get easier, and you will become aware of just how programmed we are.

Over the years I dealt with anxiety I came to understand that most of the time it was habitual. In other words, I was recreating the same fears by allowing the same story to repeat over and over in my mind.

This exercise helped me break old habitual patterns. It will do the same for you.

Fears and doubts begin with thoughts. Thoughts enter through our conscious mind. Our conscious mind is our "thinking" mind. This is where our intellect resides. But we have the ability at any given time to either accept our thoughts, or reject them. My goal is to help you learn to become "thought conscious" so you can begin to reject the negative thoughts and immediately replace them with a positive thought that will serve you.

This takes time, patience, understanding, and repetition. If you are willing to do the work, not only will you learn to heal your anxious feelings, your entire life will improve in areas from relationships to health and success.

Morning

____

____

____

____

____

Afternoon

Evening

Day 2: 10 Minute Breathing Exercise

Schedule 10 minutes two times today to sit quietly and breathe. Turn off all devices and find a comfortable spot where you can relax and simply be.

Sit up straight and relax all the muscles in your body, especially your belly. Let it hang out. Imagine Buddha's belly, really relaxed.

For the next 10 minutes your only job is to focus on the sound of your breathing. Inhale through your nose and exhale out of your mouth. Pay attention to the sounds as the breath enters your nostrils and exits your mouth.

Thoughts will come in, and that's okay. Psychologists tell us that we experience over 60,000 thoughts per day; some of which make absolutely no sense. It's normal! Just try and allow each thought to exit your mind with ease. In other words, don't get attached to these thoughts. Let them go.

This breathing exercise will bring peace, balance, and relaxation to your day. I encourage you to make it part of your daily routine.

I replaced logging onto social media with this exercise. You'd be amazed at how much extra time you have for self-care when you take a break from the distractions of social media or television. To heal from anxiety, self-love and care must be a priority over these distractions.

*Repeat Day 1 and Day 2 exercises as often as possible. Repetition is the key to your success!

Day 3: Writing Exercise

Exercise 1:

What are you feeling anxious, negative or fearful about? Write it out in detail on a blank piece of paper. Be as honest with yourself as possible.

Exercise 2:

Now, flip this situation over to the positive. Using the present tense, write how you'd like the situation to be as if it has already manifested that way in your life. (Again, it may seem silly, but we have to reprogram those old thoughts that aren't serving you!)

____

____

____

____

____

Go back to the first section where I asked you to write what you were feeling anxious about on the separate sheet of paper and tear it up! It's kind of symbolic as we want to quit focusing on and giving energy to the things and situations that are not serving us in a positive way.

Rewrite the positive outcome or the outcome you desire on a blank piece of paper ten times today.

Write out this positive outcome ten times every day for the next seven days.

Doing this will help you focus your thoughts and attention on outcomes you desire, rather than focusing on negativity and worries.

Remember, worrying is like praying for what you don't want to happen. What we focus on expands, so we must be cautious about what thoughts we allow to entertain our beautiful minds.

We choose what we entertain!

Day 4: Gratitude

Take a few minutes now and write five things you are grateful for.

____

____

____

____

____

This exercise is the quickest way to get your mind out of a state of anxiousness, worry, fear or doubt and redirected onto a path of wellness.

Gratitude journaling raises your vibration and put things into perspective. It keeps us centered and in the present moment.

You've probably heard about being, and living in the "present" moment.

When I first heard this term, long before I became a yoga instructor, I remember being a little confused. I really couldn't grasp what it meant.

This is the best way I can explain it today to someone who may be feeling as if it's a "cliché quote" like I once did:

We can't live in the past because the past is over. Therefore, it doesn't even exist. At the same time, we can't worry about the future because, like the past, it doesn't exist. All we have is this moment that's right in front of us. This is the present. Living in this space is pure bliss.

I like to ask my students this question: If we spend most of our time holding grudges about our past or being fearful and anxious about the future, when do we live?

The answer is we don't. There is no living in those places. Life only exists in the now.

One of the first things I do each morning is write in my gratitude journal for this reason. It keeps me focused on the present.

Another thing I love to do is think about things I'd like to manifest in my life and write them in my gratitude journal in the present tense as if they've already come true. You can do this for anything you desire. This is a key component to manifesting your desires. You have to fuse with your desires and act as if they've already come true in your life.

If healing anxiety is what you want for your life you can write this:

"I am so happy and grateful that I am calm, peaceful, and confident all of the time."

Write that statement five times below.

____

____

____

____

____

You can use this practice for acquiring wealth, releasing weight or anything you desire. Have some fun with it!

Day 5: Forgiveness

I know this is hard sometimes, but ask yourself this question:

Am I ready to change my life for the better?

I bet you are if you're reading this book.

It's time to forgive. Remember, forgiving releases you from a prison you may not realize you are in.

Caution: Most likely, you will think the next exercise I'm going to ask you to do is ridiculous. I remember the first time I did it. I thought to myself, "You've got to be kidding me!"

Fast forward one year; I now have complete peace of mind with a few people I needed to forgive. I was giving these people too much space in my mind and doing so caused a lot of unnecessary suffering.

So please, just grin and bear it, you'll thank me later.

Exercise 1: Send LOVE to 2-3 people who are bothering you or have hurt you.

Close your eyes each day and imagine sending love and positivity to anyone who has hurt you or is just plain getting on your nerves.

Forgiving does not excuse another person's behavior. It also doesn't mean that you should allow people to walk all over you. True forgiveness is for your wellbeing.

Remember, what you put out; you get back.

Stop allowing others to rent space in your mind. Let it go.

Exercise 2: Send LOVE to YOU

Now, this was the hardest for me, and I think it is for most people. I've always found it easier to forgive others than to forgive myself, but this was the *game changer* in my own personal growth and understanding. When I began forgiving myself and loving myself for who God created me to be, my anxiety began to settle and a new sense of self-confidence took over.

I believe many of us suffer from anxiety for numerous reasons, but when you are confident, fears, worries, and doubt are immediately replaced with faith and understanding.

Day 6 is going to shed more light on this as I explain our mind and thoughts in more detail.

Day 6: Understanding Your Mind

Our minds are extremely impressionable, so it is very important that we learn to become aware of our thoughts and begin to replace the negative, fearful thoughts with positive thoughts that serve us better.

Fearful thoughts can turn on our flight-or-fight response. This is located in the part of the brain called the Amygdala. When faced with a threatening situation or frightful thought our Thalamus, which receives incoming stimuli, sends signals to the Amygdala and Cortex. If the Amygdala senses danger (real or perceived) it makes a quick decision and begins the flight-or-fight response. In this state our brain releases stress hormones that course though our bodies. These stress hormones are cortisol and adrenaline. This is when our hearts start racing, hands begin to sweat and shake, our blood pressure increases and we feel overwhelming doom.

Now, this isn't always a bad thing. Our fight-or-flight response is needed in times of real danger, but the problem is that in our hectic world we are living in these stressed states too much and its wreaking havoc on our bodies in the form of disease. Disease occurs when our bodies are not in ease, hence disease.

Once we understand that our beliefs are just simply thoughts we keep telling ourselves, and at any given moment we can reject a negative thought and replace it with a better thought we become masters of our minds rather than slaves to our habitual negative thinking.

Every thought we have causes an emotional reaction in the mind and a physical reaction in the body. Once we understand this we can become more mindful of which thoughts are healing and improving our lives, and which thoughts are causing us sickness and unease.

Day 7: Goals

I often think the root of our fear lies in not being honest enough with ourselves to ask what we want out of life. When was the last time you sat down and thought about all the areas of your life and then asked yourself, "What do I really want?"

For me, I lived most of my adult life worrying about what others thought about me or what others wanted me to do or become.

I remember feeling an internal conflict inside my mind. All I ever wanted to do was help others. I was born with this strong sense of nurturing and empathy for people. My family didn't always understand this desire, and they encouraged me to do things that were going to benefit me financially, using skills I never felt would help me live up to my purpose.

I went back and forth for years in my mind until one day I was in a Personal Development seminar and they asked us this question:

"What Do You Really Want?"

At that moment I realized I didn't have an answer to that question. I knew on the surface that I wanted to be free of anxiety, earn more money, lose a few pounds, and pay off my debt, but the people facilitating the seminar wanted us to go deeper than the superficial needs and desires of our life as they were in that moment.

I wrote down a goal as suggested on the goal card they provided in the seminar and began reading it every day. But that question of what I really wanted stuck in my mind, and for the next three months I tried figuring it out. I couldn't believe how hard this was.

What Do You Want?

Use an index card and write down your greatest goal. If healing from anxiety is on your list, start your sentence like this:

"I am so delighted and grateful now that I am calm all of the time. Peace of mind is one of the beautiful jewels of life."

Now, on another index card write down a big goal you have for your life.

You don't need to worry about how you are going to achieve it; just set the goal, write it down as if it has already manifested, and read that goal every single day; morning, noon and night.

Day 8: Tapping

Sit comfortably and tap on a couple meridian points to lower your stress. My favorites are located just under your collar bones (Clavicle), and the bones just underneath your eyes. Gently tap on these areas anytime you feel stressed or feel anxiety coming on. These meridian points have been used for thousands of years in acupuncture and have been scientifically proven to reduce the stress hormone cortisol which is one of the hormones that course through our bodies during an anxiety attack.

Day 9: Repetition

Today we are going to return to Day 3 and do the second part of the exercise again. Rewrite what you want and how you want the situation to unfold in the positive, but this time write it in the present tense as if it has already manifested in your life.

For example:

I am so happy and grateful now that I live in a calm and healthy state of mind. I am at peace, and I am safe. I am so happy and grateful now that {insert the good you want to acquire in your life here}.

Keep this lying around in a place where you will read it often. I keep a copy on my nightstand and desk and read it every morning as soon as I wake up and every evening before I fall asleep.

I cannot stress enough the importance of repetition. To break old patterns that have been holding us back and causing us so much fear and anxiety, we must reprogram our subconscious minds.

Day 10: Conscious Breathing

Breathing is our life force, yet the way we breathe can be a double-edged sword. Many of us are shallow breathers. I know I can be. Shallow breathing contributes to the symptoms of anxiety while deep, conscious breathing can alleviate them.

Being conscious of your breathing pattern can reduce and stop the symptoms of a panic attack, but unfortunately, many suffering a panic attack become short of breath.

I've learned that when I'm conscious of my breathing, I remain calm and relaxed. When I become overwhelmed or stressed with things to do or I have too much on my plate, I begin to hold my breath or begin shallow breathing which leads to…you guessed it, a panic or anxiety attack.

Find a comfortable place to sit. Make sure you sit up straight because slouching can compress the lungs and we want full access to both the lower and upper part of your lungs.

Take a deep cleansing breath in through your nose and exhale out through your mouth with an audible sound like a nice sigh of relief.

Do this 3 times per day or as often as you can!

Day 11: Visualize

Today we are going to visualize living fearlessly – void of any anxiety, worry, or doubt.

Exercise:

Three times today, sit or lie comfortably. Turn off all devices and distractions.

Now, daydream and feel with your body what it would be like to live without fear, worry or doubt.

Fuse with the emotion of being a calm, healthy, fearless being.

This is your birthright. You are that!

Day 12: Extra Grateful

Today, write 20 things you're grateful for that already exist in your life, and 20 things you'd like to manifest.

Write the things you'd like to have manifest in the present tense as if they've already manifested.

Read each one and take a moment to feel what it would be like to have that desire.

Day 13: Your Dream Life

Write your dream life. Over the next 24 hours sit down and write a new script for your life. Cover all aspects including family, health, success, relationships and spiritual. Make sure to include being calm and having peace of mind.

This is a very powerful exercise if you are serious about changing your current circumstances. It's also fun! Go into your marvelous mind and imagine the life you truly want to live. You are an abundant being. We live in an abundant universe. Sometimes we just need to shift our perception from a lack mentality to an abundance mentality. I want to help you achieve this.

Take your time with this exercise. Try and be as detailed as possible. This was a hard exercise in the beginning. I was startled to realize I didn't know exactly what I wanted. I knew I wanted to be free of anxiety and fear thoughts, and I wanted to make more money and give my children a better future without their mom struggling to make ends meet.

Today, three years later, I've learned all these tools and they help me daily, I'm no longer struggling financially, and I've written a book! This was all written in my new script for my life.

Here's the best news of all. You don't have to know how you are going to accomplish any of your new goals. All you need to do is imagine and BELIEVE, take action, and embody the feeling of your goal or desire already being achieved. The Universe will begin to work for the fulfillment of your desires.

I learned this from my Mentor, Peggy McColl. She has a fantastic resource that teaches you exactly how to write your script at www.powerlifescript.com. Check it out! She's amazing.

Day 14: Record Your Dream Life

Record Your Dream Life.

Today, record your "New Dream Life" with enthusiasm as if it's already manifested into your life. Listen to it every day in the morning and evening before bed.

Some readers might be thinking "this is just weird", and I felt the same way at first, but it's about reprogramming those old limiting beliefs that have been holding you back. You deserve a wonderful life! Once you begin playing your recording repeatedly, you'll be amazed at the changes that begin to take place in your life.

Day 15: Recap

By now I hope you are beginning to understand these things:

- You don't have to live with the symptoms of anxiety
- Fear manifests itself from the mind into the body as anxiety
- Fears are beliefs we continue to tell ourselves
- Fears are just thoughts
- At any time, you can change your thoughts
- We need only to focus on the results we want
- Continue to scribble away anything that doesn't reflect what you want from the lesson on Day 2
- Gratitude is the best attitude
- Forgiveness is the key to peace and happiness
- YOU ARE SAFE!

Day 16: Conscious Thinking

As often as possible today, be aware of your thoughts. Psychologists tell us that the average human has anywhere from 60,000 to 70,000 thoughts per day. That's a lot of thinking!

If you spent time simply being conscious of your thoughts, you would realize that most of them are repetitive and or negative. This practice will help you eliminate negative thoughts.

For today's exercise, relax and pay attention throughout the day to what's going on in your mind. If you catch yourself with a negative thought pattern just accept it for what it is and let the thoughts flow away. Imagine your mind as the blue sky and your thoughts as white clouds passing by.

Day 17: De-Clutter Your Space

It has been scientifically proven that clutter induces stress and anxiety. Clutter can be defined as having an overwhelming amount of possessions in our homes, offices, storage spaces and even vehicles. Clutter creates stress that has three major neurological and biological effects on individuals. It affects our cortisol levels, our creativity and ability to focus, and our experience of pain.

Today, start somewhere, even if it's just putting a plan in place or writing a list of "to-dos". Sometimes clutter can be so overwhelming you don't know where to start. Start with a drawer or closet and commit to cleaning and clearing some clutter every day or each week.

You deserve to live in a clean and comfortable environment that relaxes you, rather than one that stresses you. You'll feel so much more peaceful and energized!

Day 18: Spend Time in Nature

Spend time outdoors today in nature. A growing body of research has explored the idea that nature brings serenity. As little as five minutes per day is beneficial. Sit and watch the clouds, the birds, the trees and breathe in some fresh air. Nature is not only our greatest teacher, it is also extremely therapeutic.

Day 19: Take a 10 Minute Walk

Today, find 10 minutes to take a walk while repeating this powerful affirmation:

"All the stress I've been carrying around...with every step, I'll leave it behind, clear my mind, and fuel my soul."

Day 20: Serve Others

There are so many ways we can serve others in this life. Today, try smiling at a stranger, give a genuine compliment to someone you run into, listen intently to your friend's problem or volunteer in your community or at church. There is no better feeling than to help others.

Day 21: Reach out to someone you Love

Reach out to a friend or relative you haven't spoken to in a while. You could do this with a special note or by phone. Maybe plan a lunch date.

I believe technology and the lack of human intimacy is partially responsible for the rise of anxiety and depression. We were created to interact and love and support one another. While technology has made life easier in many ways, like everything else, there should be a balance.

Day 22: Make a music playlist

Create a playlist of soothing and upbeat songs you can play each morning and evening to help keep your mind calm and happy.

Music has been used for hundreds of years to restore harmony in the mind and body. However, it is important to choose music that is soothing to you and lifts your spirits.

Day 23: More Gratitude

With your non-dominant hand, write 20 things you are grateful for.

Day 24: Box Breathing

Box breathing, also known as square breathing, is a technique used when taking slow deep breaths. It is a very powerful stress reliever. It is beneficial for anyone, especially those suffering with anxiety. It is used by Navy SEALs, fire fighters, police officers, people in the medical field, and athletes.

Sit up straight and exhale to a count of four, then hold and pause your breath for a count of four, now inhale to a count of four, then once again hold and pause your breath for a count of four. Do this a minimum of 5 times.

Day 25: More Repetition

Seven times throughout the day today, read the New Dream Life you created on Day 13.

Day 26: Listen to Your New Dream Life Recording

Listen to your new dream life script three times throughout the day.

Day 27: Believe that you are free from anxiety!

Whatever you believe about yourself on the inside is what you will manifest on the outside.

Believe you are free from anxiety!

Believe in your dreams!

Believe you are worthy of all the greatness you desire!

Your belief will create the fact. I repeat….Your belief will create the fact!

Day 28: Reevaluate Who You Are and What You Want

Sit quietly today with a piece of paper and reevaluate your wants, desires, dreams, career path, path of service and anything else you desire in life. This is very powerful because if we don't know what we desire in life, we are living on auto pilot and potentially robbing ourselves of a wonderful life. You are full of potential! Stretch and you'll reach your highest goals!

Day 29: Think Better, Live Better

Be aware today of any negative or fearful thoughts and quickly replace them with their positive aspect. For example; if you have an exam coming up and a thought enters your mind such as "I'm going to fail this exam." Replace it with this thought, "I am so delighted and grateful now that I've passed my exam!" or "I am so happy I am going to rock that exam!"

Day 30: Be Your Own Best Friend

Be aware throughout today, and every day, of how you speak to yourself.

It's not your fault you have negative self-talk. This was programmed into your subconscious mind either by relatives at an early age, society, media or just one bologna thought that you've had on auto loop for the past 10-20 years.

Whatever the case, it's okay! Just recognize they are just thoughts that have become beliefs that *no longer* and *never did* serve you.

Treat yourself like you treat your own best friend. Encourage yourself, praise your beautiful self, appreciate your creativity, your body, and all of the mountains you climbed to get to where you are now.

Your 100 Day Gratitude Journal

& Daily Affirmations for Cultivating Abundance and an Attitude of Gratitude

"What are 10 things you are grateful for today?"

“What are 5 things that you love?”

"In the present tense white 10 things you'd like to manifest in your life."

"I AM happy and grateful now that {Insert your good}"

"I AM Divinely Guided"

"Sometimes it's just about the little things in life like clean running water. What are 10 little things you are grateful for today?"

"Rampage of Gratitude"

“Interrupt Anxiety with Gratitude”

"With Gratitude I Create a Peaceful Abundant Life"

~Denise Lynn

"List 5 things you are joyful about."

"Life is meant to be fun for you! What are 10 fun things you want to do this week?"

“Bless others. Who is on your heart today? Bless them now.”

"List 5 things you appreciate about yourself."

"I AM deeply aware that what I put out multiplies.
Today I am grateful for. . ."

“Inhale love. Exhale love.”

"I AM so happy and appreciative now that money comes to me in increasing quantities through multiple sources on a continuous basis."

"I release all fears, doubts and indecision from my consciousness."

"I'm sorry, please forgive me, thank you, I love you" . . . An Ancient Hawaiian Healing Prayer, Ho'oponopono.

"We are often programmed to see and think and feel about things that aren't going right in our lives. Today let's focus on what's going well because what we focus on expands."

~Denise Lynn

"I AM so happy and grateful now that I am choosing better thoughts and when I am thinking better I'm feeling better."

~Denise Lynn

"Love is Life"

"Fill your mind and this page with these words: Fun, Love, Joy, Happiness, Peace and Contribution"

"Life is what YOU make of it."

"Forgiveness is the key to happiness. . . for others and especially for ourselves." ~Denise Lynn

"I look forward to the happy expectancy of this day."

"Make Today Amazing"

"Something wonder-full is going to happen today!"

~Denise Lynn

"I AM abundant and I live in an abundant universe."

"Pay Attention to your thoughts today because we really do become what we think about." ~Denise Lynn

“You are powerfully creative.”

"Return to love, peace and forgiveness" ~Denise Lynn

"Forgive yourself. We all make errors. Just don't do it again. It's that simple." ~Denise Lynn

"God, how can I serve you today?"

"God is the source of my supply and all my needs are met every day."

"I AM calm and serene."

"I AM so happy and grateful that I have clean water to drink."

“Everything is always working out for me.”

“I AM Abundant!”

"Do one good deed a day."

"I AM Love. I AM Confident. I AM Healthy."

"Imagination Creates Reality."

"Always look for things to appreciate." ~Denise Lynn

"Thank you God, for this beautiful day!"

“I Love. I Give. I Receive.”

"Let it go."

"Thank you is the greatest prayer."~Denise Lynn

"I am grateful for the ability to choose which thoughts I want to entertain." ~Denise Lynn

"I AM free to think whatever I choose."

"Think better, live better."

"You'll have no chance unless you take one."

“Forgiveness is a great healer.”

"I attract abundance into my life."

"See, feel & believe."

"Send love to others daily."

"There will be a day that people will learn and just know that their thoughts are what's controlling their lives."

~Denise Lynn

“I AM grateful for my breath.”

"Just Breathe"

"Thank you God for another day."

“Abundance is my birthright.”

"You've got to have faith."

"YOU are amazing."

“YOU are enough.”

"Surrender your fears to God."

"Abundance is everywhere. Look at the leaves in the trees, the abundance of grass, and the birds in the sky."

~Denise Lynn

"You are an abundant being worthy of all the good you desire." ~Denise Lynn

"Today is going to be a great day!"

"Rehearse the greatest version of yourself every day."

"Good thinking paves the way to a happy fulfilling life."~Denise Lynn

"There is no healing without forgiveness and love. For others and especially for ourselves." ~Denise Lynn

"Decide you are worthy, focus on contribution, increase your value and express your love." ~Denise Lynn

"There are no risks involved in trying to reach the best state of mind possible." ~Denise Lynn

"Thank you for this lovely day."

"Move forward in love."

“I AM a divine magnificent creation of God.”

"Expand your awareness every day."

"If you desire a thing you already have what's needed to attain it but you do have to match its frequency. Vibe higher." ~Denise Lynn

"What other people think about you is none of your business. What matters is what YOU think of YOU." ~Denise Lynn

"Send anyone who is annoying you love. Just close your eyes and send them love. Stop allowing others to rent space in your mind." ~Denise Lynn

"You deserve to be happy." ~Denise Lynn

"There is always something to be grateful for."

"Believe and you will achieve."

"What are you waiting for?"

“I believe in happy endings.”

"Today at this very moment you have a blank slate. You can rewrite your future today!" ~Denise Lynn

"I AM grateful. I AM so extremely grateful."

"I AM blessed beyond measure."

"Happiness is not a destination. It's a state of mind."

~Denise Lynn

“We receive our breath from God then we give it away. Focus for a moment on that. Focus on your breath and give thanks.” ~Denise Lynn

"I AM too blessed to be stressed."

"Take it Easy"

"I AM Confident"

"I AM Lovable"

"What I Desire, Desires ME"

“Feeling is the secret”

"Keys to manifesting your desires: think, feel, act as if and BELIEVE"

"Gratitude turns what we already have into enough and makes room for more to come." ~Denise Lynn

"Let's be grateful for the people that make us happy."

~Denise Lynn

“With God and Myself all things are possible.”

"Piglet noticed that even though he had a Very Small Heart it could hold a rather large amount of gratitude,"

~AA Milne Winnie-the-Pooh

"Thank you, God for this beautiful day. It is God's day. I AM poised, serene and calm."

Made in the USA
Columbia, SC
02 June 2021

38866522R00088